IMAGES OF MYSTIC SEAPORT

IMAGES OF MYSTIC SEAPORT

the photographs of Oliver Denison III

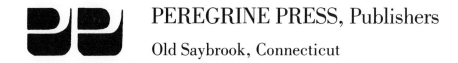

PEREGRINE PRESS, Publishers

Old Saybrook, Connecticut

This book is dedicated to Nancy, David, Deborah and William for their patience and understanding in waiting around for me to take pictures or to come out of the darkroom.

COVER: Christmastime

Designed by Susan Hildebrandt

Mystic Seaport is a registered trademark of Mystic Seaport Museum, Inc.

Manufactured in the United States of America

First Printing

ISBN 0–933614–01–2

INTRODUCTION

Mystic Seaport Museum is many things to many people, but for anyone who has ever been here, it is a singularly magical experience. For gathered here, in one historic setting, are all the equipage, accoutrements, and trappings of America's dramatic seafaring history. The ships themselves, ranging from the famous whaleship *Charles W. Morgan* and the square-rigged *Joseph Conrad* to a collection of more than 200 smaller boats, represent the wide variety of vessels developed and used in this country. More than 60 buildings on the 40-acre complex house businesses, crafts, and industries that were required to supply and support the ships. The historic ships, exhibits, and buildings create the atmosphere of an almost lost piece of American history, wonderfully and faithfully preserved for this and future generations. It is a trip into the past and, we hope, a guide for the future. A life connected with the sea was sometimes bitterly hard, yet it had a delightful simplicity and rhythm about it. The adaptability, ingenuity, and frequent humor of these hardy seafaring folk can certainly be a lesson for our bustling, and sometimes uncaring, twentieth-century society.

But overriding all this, at least in the mind of the photographer, is the fact that Mystic Seaport is a great place to take pictures. The variety of material is surprising, even to those who have some knowledge about the place. Of course there are the big ships themselves, but in addition there are many smaller craft afloat or ashore that make attractive subjects for a camera. The exterior of many of the buildings, singly or in a group, is picturesque and the rooms and objects inside are equally worthy of attention. A close-up view of some detail may be even more pictorial than a view of a whole building or vessel.

It is a place of many moods, depending on the time of year, the time of day, and the weather. While some of the small craft must be put away or covered up during the winter, the larger ships are always on view even during a snowstorm. A foggy day is one of the most popular times to be here with a camera: the nearby scene stands out against the muted background in a most attractive manner. Early morning is usually best for reflections in the river, before the breeze creates too many ripples or waves, but conditions are often good in the evening as long as the light lasts.

And there is most always some sort of activity going on. During much of the year staff members are demonstrating the setting or furling of a sail aloft on one of the square riggers, rowing or sailing one of the small boats, using the breeches buoy rescue training apparatus, or showing how to clean and dry fish. Indoors, others will be cooking on a stove or at a fireplace, weaving fabric on a loom, sewing a sail, or heating and hammering iron in the shipsmith's shop. In the shipyard area, shipwrights and painters will be going about the never-ending business of restoring and maintaining vessels of all sizes. Picture-taking opportunities seem endless.

This book displays only black and white photographs. While the Seaport is also a great place to shoot color pictures, the old-fashioned atmosphere of much of it lends itself to monochrome portrayal. Cameras with wide angle and telephoto lenses may capture a greater variety of subjects, but much can be done with simple equipment. For example, the picture captioned "Corner of the Chandlery" was taken in the building using a pocket Instamatic, and the tiny 110 size negative has also been enlarged to make a very satisfactory 11 x 14 inch print. Fast film is a help in the rather dark interiors, but tripods are allowed in most places; this permits shooting with slower film as long as the camera shutter is capable of longer exposures. Except for the 110 picture mentioned above, all the others in this book are from 35 mm negatives. Kodak Tri-X was used more than any other kind of film, with development in D-76.

I have had the pleasure of being associated with Mystic Seaport Museum since 1951 (in the accounting and administrative offices), and thus have had frequent opportunities to practice my hobby of photography at this fascinating place. It seems that there is always something new or different to consider for a photograph, even after these many years. The wealth of subjects to photograph only reflects the wealth of images perceived, and Mystic Seaport has enough for many lifetimes.

Oliver Denison III
Mystic, Connecticut

Friendship sloop ▶

Arrival of Charles W. Morgan — *1941*

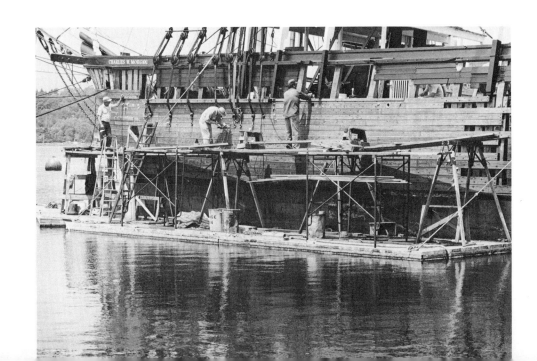

Replanking

Charles W. Morgan

Old cart

◄ Rigging Loft

Solitary

Cobblestone street

Sails ▶

Lobster shack

Figurehead, Joseph Conrad

Spring painting

*Lanterns and
running lights*

Joseph Conrad ▶

Nellie

Winter ▶

Caulking

Lighthouse

◄ *In the fog*

Old glass

Icebound

Snowstorm

Ropewalk

White fence

Dories and whaleboat

◄ *Oyster House*

Ship painter

◀ *Along the waterfront*

Seaport Street

Estella A.

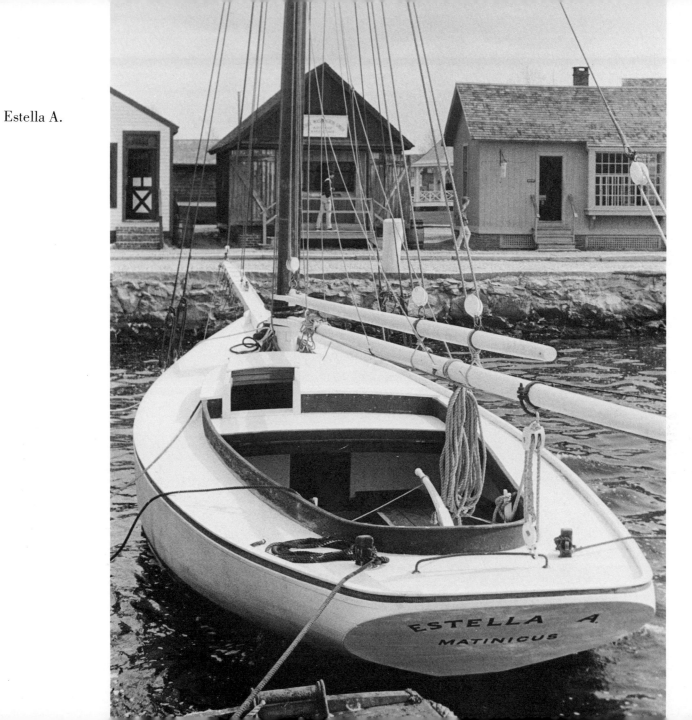

Twins

Noble Figure

Shipcarver's shop

Corner of the Chandlery

◀ *Bowsprit*

Early morning

Edwards House

Dories

Middle Wharf

Tools

Block ▶

Chandlery

Deadeyes

◄ *Capstans*

The Sabino

Small Boat Shop

Spinning Room

Rudderhead "Saucy Sally"

General Store

Buckingham House

Visitor

Anchor